Dragonflies

by Cheryl Coughlan

Consulting Editor: Gail Saunders-Smith, Ph.D.

Consultant: Gary A. Dunn, Director of Education,
Young Entomologists' Society

Pebble Books

an imprint of Capstone Press
Mankato, Minnesota

Pebble Books are published by Capstone Press
1710 Roe Crest Drive, North Mankato, Minnesota 56003
www.capstonepub.com

Library of Congress Cataloging-in-Publication Data
Coughlan, Cheryl.
    Dragonflies/by Cheryl Coughlan.
    p. cm.—(Insects)
    Includes bibliographical references (p. 23) and index.
    Summary: Simple text and photographs introduce the physical features
of dragonflies.
    ISBN-13: 978-0-7368-0238-3 (hardcover)
    ISBN-10: 0-7368-0238-X (hardcover)
    ISBN-13: 978-0-7368-8209-5 (softcover pbk.)
    ISBN-10: 0-7368-8209-X (softcover pbk.)
    1. Dragonflies—Juvenile literature. [1. Dragonflies.] I. Title. II. Series: Insects
(Mankato, Minn.)
QL520.C685 1999
595.7'33—dc21

                                                                    98-32304

Note to Parents and Teachers

The Insects series supports national science standards for units on the
diversity and unity of life. The series shows that animals have features that
help them live in different environments. This book describes and
illustrates the parts of dragonflies. The photographs support early readers
in understanding the text. The repetition of words and phrases helps early
readers learn new words. This book also introduces early readers to
subject-specific vocabulary words, which are defined in the Words to Know
section. Early readers may need assistance to read some words and to use
the Table of Contents, Words to Know, Read More, Internet Sites, and
Index/Word List sections of the book.

Printed in the United States of America in North Mankato, Minnesota.
052015
008968R

Table of Contents

Dragonflies live near water.

Dragonflies can be colorful.

8

Dragonflies have
a long body.

Dragonflies have six legs.

Dragonflies have four wings.

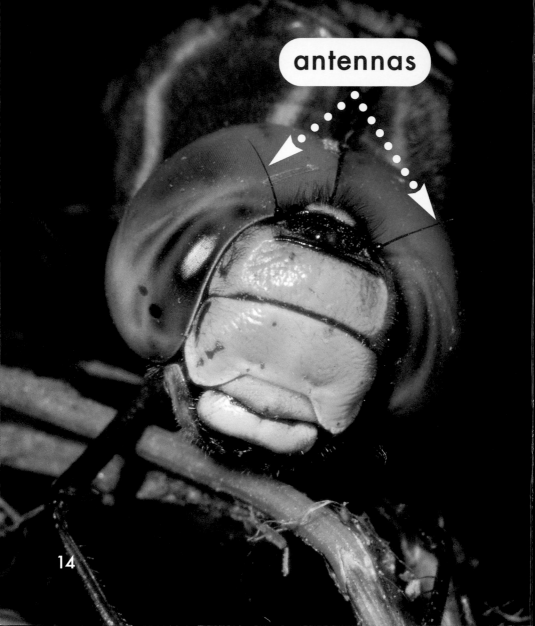

antennas

Dragonflies have
two short antennas.

Dragonflies have
two huge eyes.

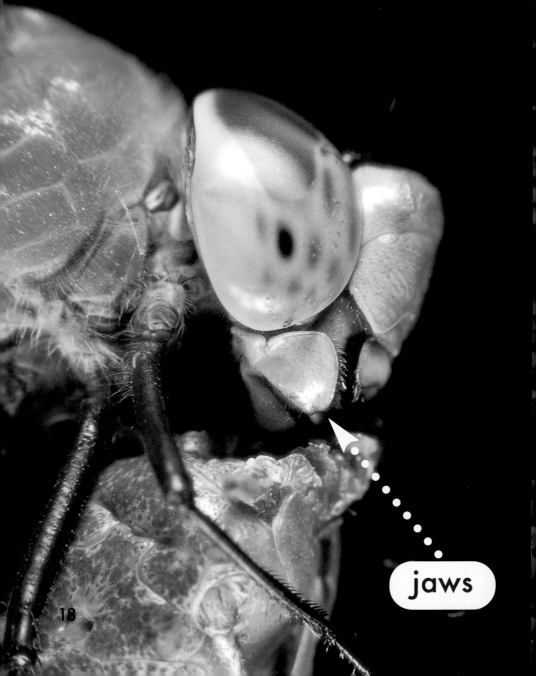

jaws

Dragonflies have strong jaws.

20

Dragonflies eat
other insects.

Words to Know

antenna—a feeler on an insect's head

eye—a body part used for seeing; dragonflies have large eyes made of many small lenses; dragonflies can see in nearly all directions at the same time.

insect—a small animal with a hard outer shell, three body parts, six legs, and two antennas; insects may have two or four wings.

jaw—a mouthpart used to grab things, bite, and chew; dragonflies use their jaws to catch and eat insects such as flies, gnats, and mosquitoes.

wing—a movable part of an insect that helps it fly; dragonflies have clear, tinted, or spotted wings.

Read More

Green, Jen. *Dragonflies.* Nature's Children. Danbury, Conn.: Grolier Educational, 1999.

Jacobs, Liza. *Dragonflies.* Wild Wild World. San Diego: Blackbirch Press, 2003.

Meister, Cari. *Dragonflies.* Insects. Edina, Minn: Abdo, 2001.

Morris, Ting. *Dragonfly.* North Mankato, Minn.: Smart Apple Media, 2003.

Internet Sites

FactHound offers a safe, fun way to find Internet sites related to this book. All of the sites on FactHound have been researched by our staff.
Here's how:
1. Visit *www.facthound.com.*
2. Type in this special code **073680238X** for age-appropriate sites. Or enter a search word related to this book for a more general search.
3. Click on the **Fetch It** button.
FactHound will fetch the best sites for you!

23

Index/Word List

Word Count: 39
Early-Intervention Level: 7

Editorial Credits

Mari C. Schuh, editor; Timothy Halldin, cover designer; Kimberly Danger and
   Sheri Gosewisch, photo researchers

Photo Credits

Dembinsky Photo Assoc. Inc./Gary Meszaros, 4
Fred Siskind, 6
GeoIMAGERY/Jim Roetzel, 10
James P. Rowan, cover
Joe MacDonald, 1, 12, 14
Susan Fay, 8
Unicorn Stock Photos/Ed Harp, 16
Visuals Unlimited/Bill Beatty, 18; Mary Meszaros, 20